The official seal of The Statue of Liberty-Ellis Island Foundation, Inc.
crafted from genuine 22 karat gold.

A Celebration of Freedom

LIBERTY WEEKEND 1986

A CELEBRATION OF FREEDOM

LIBERTY WEEKEND 1986

LIBERTY CENTENNIAL PRESS
WESTPORT, CONNECTICUT

Publisher's Preface

What a party it was! From the dramatic relighting of Liberty's torch on July 3 to the spectacular finale of the Closing Ceremonies on July 6, Liberty Weekend 1986 was America's tribute to the Statue of Liberty. It was the celebration of a lifetime. Liberty Weekend came off without a hitch — the magnificent Tall Ships of Operation Sail 1986, the brass bands and parades, the Harbor Festival's street fair, and the incredible fireworks display were perfectly planned and executed. The dazzling star-spangled Closing Ceremonies were a stunning finale to the festivities. For those millions who saw the Weekend, either as spectators in New York City or as TV viewers across the nation and around the world, it will remain a precious patriotic memory.

This special commemorative volume has been designed to allow you to recall and relive the historic Weekend forever, preserving both the spirit and the spectacle of this great tribute to our most beloved symbol of freedom. Every effort has been taken to make this edition a volume that you and your family will always treasure. Many thousands of photographs of the Statue of Liberty and the gala events of Liberty Weekend were painstakingly reviewed to insure that only the best and most exciting would be included within these pages. *A Celebration of Freedom-Liberty Weekend 1986* will keep these stirring events alive for yourself, your children, and future generations.

The Liberty Centennial Press gratefully acknowledges the important assistance provided by several individuals and organizations. It was with the help of The Statue of Liberty-Ellis Island Foundation, Inc., chaired by Lee A. Iacocca, that *A Celebration of Freedom* was published.

David L. Wolper and the Liberty Weekend 1986 Committee's tireless efforts brought America the greatest party the nation has ever seen. The grandeur and excitement of America's four-day party was planned and engineered by David Wolper and his Liberty Weekend staff. All that was promised came to fruition — plus many, many delightful surprises.

The vision and skills of Peter B. Kaplan Images, Ltd. enabled us to preserve and present so many of the spectacular photographs within this volume. The Kaplan team was virtually everywhere during Liberty Weekend, capturing forever on film the memories of a lifetime.

Adding words and additional color to these great sights is the informative narrative of David Roberts. His work adds a special "inside" perspective to this historical event.

The relighting and reopening of the Statue of Liberty were very special events and *A Celebration of Freedom* is a very special book that captures these historic moments. As you look at the magnificent photographs and read the informative narrative you will recall all the excitement and glory that was America's greatest celebration — Liberty Weekend 1986.

Douglas Mac John
The Liberty Centennial Press

Lee A. Iacocca and his mother on Ellis Island.

A Personal Message from
Lee A. Iacocca

The Statue of Liberty was the first American landmark for the millions of immigrants who landed at Ellis Island between 1892 and 1954. To the hundred million of us who are their children, the Lady with the torch remains a symbol of what those people and this country gave to us. During Liberty Weekend, we gave something back.

After enduring 100 years of weather and wear, the Lady needed help. Though her spirit and meaning never tarnished, her structure required extensive restoration and repair both inside and out.

When asked to help, I was proud to do so, and when Americans were asked to help, they gave with their hearts and from their pocketbooks. From large corporations to school children, from contributions of millions of dollars to contributions of pennies, America chipped in.

On one glorious weekend we celebrated the results of those loving and patriotic contributions. We relighted the torch that inspired the millions who sought the refuge of democracy and the chance to live and raise their families with dignity and in liberty.

On Liberty Weekend we were proud — proud of our country and of our countrymen, proud of what we have and of what we've earned, and proud of what our efforts had done to insure that the Lady will always stand and continue to offer hope and liberty to ourselves and to the world.

Within the pages of this book, *A Celebration of Freedom,* the events of Liberty Weekend 1986 are faithfully recorded in words and photographs. American hearts were touched with thoughts of our great country during four memorable days. This book will help to keep the excitement, patriotism, and joy of the celebration alive forever.

Everyone who helped to make the restoration and the celebration possible has earned the thanks of all Americans and my personal gratitude.

Lee A. Iacocca
Chairman, The Statue of Liberty-
Ellis Island Foundation, Inc.

David L. Wolper

*Chairman and Executive Producer of
Liberty Weekend 1986*

As the Chairman and Executive Producer of Liberty Weekend 1986, David L. Wolper coordinated the planning and staging of every event, from the Opening Ceremonies on the evening of July 3, 1986, through the Closing Ceremonies on July 6, 1986.

An internationally renowned filmmaker, Wolper brought the Emmy Award-winning *Roots* to television screens around the world, and produced the spectacular Opening and Closing Ceremonies of the 1984 Olympic Games in Los Angeles.

The creator of over 500 films, Wolper has won more than 150 awards, including two Oscars, 40 Emmys, seven Golden Globes, three Freedom Foundation Awards and five Peabodys. Many of the world's great film festivals have presented retrospectives of his work.

Wolper was one of seven men responsible for bringing the Olympic Games to Los Angeles. He was a vice-chairman of the Los Angeles Olympic Organizing Committee and a member of the Board of Directors Executive Committee. As Chairman of the Television Commission, Wolper negotiated the unprecedented $225 million agreement with ABC network to televise the Games.

In 1958, after coming across 6,000 feet of extraordinary Soviet film documenting the Russian space program, Wolper produced the *Race for Space*. He gathered support from advertisers, but the network refused to run the program because of a policy prohibiting any independently produced documentary. Undaunted, Wolper arranged for 150 local stations, "a fourth network," to carry his film. The *Race for Space* won numerous international awards and was the first television program ever nominated for an Academy Award.

In 1967, Wolper convinced French underwater explorer Jacques Cousteau to lead an expedition around the world for a series of American television specials. He produced the highly regarded programs for five years, bringing Jacques Cousteau international acclaim.

The Hellstrom Chronicle, a study of the life cycles of insects, brought Wolper his first Oscar in 1971, after nine nominations in the documentary division. He won his second Oscar in 1985, receiving the prestigious Jean Hersholt Humanitarian Award.

Former President Gerald Ford appointed Wolper to the Advisory Council for the American Revolution Bicentennial Administration in January 1975. He was the only film industry representative named to the 25-member council and was voted chairman.

Among his 500 films, Wolper produced the miniseries *The Thorn Birds; The Rise and Fall of the Third Reich; The March of Time; Carl Sandburg's Lincoln; The Making of the President 1960* and *The Making of the President 1964.*

He is a trustee of The American Film Institute, The Los Angeles County Museum of Art, The American Federation of Arts, The Los Angeles Heart Institute and the Los Angeles Olympic Committee Amateur Athletic Foundation.

Mr. Wolper lives with his artist wife, Gloria, in Bel Air, California. He has two sons, Mark and Michael, both in the entertainment industry, and a daughter, Leslie Ann, a college student.

ABOUT THE PHOTOGRAPHY

Peter B. Kaplan and Peter B. Kaplan Images, Ltd. have provided the great majority of the spectacular photographs included in this book. No other photographer could be more qualified — for Peter B. Kaplan has devoted the past four years of his life to photographing the Statue of Liberty.

Beginning with a four-day assignment from The Statue of Liberty-Ellis Island Foundation, in August of 1982, to provide photographs for use in a 13 minute audio/visual film showing the condition of the Statue, Kaplan fell in love with freedom's great symbol. After learning of the Foundation's satisfaction with his work, he volunteered to provide photographs to be used in fund-raising efforts — and was granted the title of "Preferred Photographer" of the Foundation.

Kaplan is one of the few photographers to receive permission to climb through the Statue's superstructure. Beginning inside her right foot he worked his way up — photographing damage and decay, until he reached the top of her upraised torch. His photographs confirmed the need for repair.

Over the next four years Kaplan photographed the Lady continually — in every season and weather condition (once almost losing fingers to frost bite) and from every conceivable vantage point, sometimes using ropes to climb out over her crown.

Kaplan and workers on the restoration teams quickly developed an excellent rapport based upon his respect for their skills and efforts and theirs for his ability to work and function along with them on narrow scaffolding as high as 320 feet from the ground. At the height of the restoration activities Kaplan was spending five to six days a week, 14 hours a day, recording all work. He even travelled to remote workshops in New Jersey and upstate New York. By the time the restoration was complete, Peter B. Kaplan made over 80,000 images of the restoration.

Kaplan's photography documents the whole story: from the early testing done by engineers, through all stages of repair work, to the breathtaking events of Liberty Weekend 1986.

When the restoration work began to wind down Kaplan began to plan how he would photograph the Liberty Weekend celebration. As the details of the event began to unfold, he realized he would need to enlarge his staff in order to cover thoroughly the great number of events involved. In endless planning sessions the schedule of the festivities was reviewed, assignments given and locations chosen. Kaplan applied for, and received, permission to climb, and position photographers atop, both the Brooklyn and Manhattan bridges. During Liberty Weekend, he and his team were virtually everywhere: photographing from the World Trade Center, on fireworks barges, on Governors Island, atop the Empire State Building, aboard the John F. Kennedy aircraft carrier, in helicopters, on tugboats and barges, and interspersed among the crowds in the streets. Peter B. Kaplan, naturally, stationed himself in the command booth on Liberty Island.

Over the course of Liberty Weekend, Kaplan and his team of 24 photographers exposed 700 rolls of film — immediately rushing them, in batches, to the lab for processing. Averaging only about four and a half hours of sleep per day, they dedicated themselves to providing a complete and historic documentation of America's largest celebration. The results of that selfless work can be seen within the pages of this book. With great skill and sensitivity Peter B. Kaplan has preserved and presented all the beauty, poignancy, history and joy that was Liberty Weekend 1986.

The Gift

America's celebration of the centennial of the Statue of Liberty in July of 1986 lived up to President Reagan's prediction as the greatest party in history.

The Lady with the torch is one of the most famous monuments in the world. She is a treasured symbol of liberty and freedom to Americans; and her torch carries this powerful message to the world. Yet the Statue of Liberty came perilously close to not existing at all. At first, some Americans failed to appreciate this gift from France, while many found its design unusual. As a sculptural and engineering feat of the 1880's, the Statue's creation involved radical and brilliant solutions to design problems that had never been encountered before. When the torch was set in place in 1886, the Statue stood taller than any building in New York City. In the early years, her meaning to Americans was vague. She was intended neither as a welcoming beacon for immigrants nor as a symbol of America. At that time, she was not even called the Statue of Liberty. She was referred to as *The Statue of Liberty Enlightening the World.*

A glance at her history gives us a fresh appreciation of the Statue as she begins her second century. The idea of the Statue arose during a dinner party at a country estate in France near the Palace of Versailles in 1865, fully 21 years before the Statue was erected in New York Harbor. A French law professor and political leader, Edouard René Lefebvre de Laboulaye, often spoke of the traditions and ideals shared by many Frenchmen and the American people. As a champion of democracy, he admired America's struggle for personal liberty and the role France had played in the American Revolution. A memorial to that common ideal might be in order — a monument, perhaps, built as a common effort of the two nations.

Among Laboulaye's guests that evening was the impressionable and ambitious young sculptor Frédéric-Auguste Bartholdi. Nothing that Bartholdi had ever heard fired his zeal more than Laboulaye's idea. Gradually the monument became the sculptor's obsession. In 1871, he sailed to the United States to look for a site. Bedloe's Island in New York Harbor quickly struck his fancy. Upon his return home he began experimenting with many designs and models before settling on Liberty's final form — an imposing 151 foot colossal monument made of hammered copper. Originally, the French hoped to present the gift to America in time for the U.S. Centennial in 1876, but it proved impossible to meet such a demanding timetable given the political and fund-raising problems incurred. However, the hand and torch were completed and dis-

Finally, in 1881, after constructing the Statue in sections, Bartholdi began erecting his colossal memorial — not in New York Harbor, but in the street outside a cavernous workshop in Paris. In front of throngs of curious onlookers, the Statue — 151 feet, two inches tall — was erected in the center of Paris. Just as the French grew fond of the Lady, she was dismantled, packed carefully in crates, carried by train to Rouen, and shipped by sea in 1885 to America where she sat in boxes awaiting completion of her pedestal.

Unfortunately, in the United States, preparations for receiving the Statue had lagged behind schedule. In 1883, General Charles P. Stone took charge of the all-important job of laying a foundation for the Statue. General Stone wisely opted for concrete, but pouring a slab 91 feet square and 52 feet, 10 inches high was an unprecedented task. In order that the Statue be prominently visible, a pedestal 87 feet tall had to be built atop the foundation. However, there was not enough money available to complete the pedestal. Fortunately, Joseph Pulitzer, publisher of *The World*, used his newspaper to spearhead a national fund-raising campaign beginning in March 1885. Within five months Pulitzer coaxed citizens and firms from all over the country into donating more than $120,000, a staggering sum at that time. The average gift was under

played in Philadelphia at the Centennial Celebration.

The engineering problem of how to support the Statue was entrusted to the French master Gustave Eiffel, famous for his airy-looking and extremely stable railroad bridges and later for the great iron tower in Paris named after him. Eiffel's predecessor on the project had envisioned a massive cast sculpture supported by compartments filled with sand. However, Eiffel insisted on the use of a strong central pylon made of wrought iron. Projecting from this pylon were horizontal struts bolted to flat bars which in turn connected a spidery strapwork that conformed to the interior of the Statue's skin.

The brilliance of Eiffel's scheme was that it allowed the skin of the Statue — less than the thickness of two pennies — to float and flex, almost as if breathing, so that the tempestuous winds and extreme temperature changes of the harbor could be taken in stride. It was this feat of engineering — the first example of modern "curtain wall" construction —that anticipated the design of today's skyscraper. Eiffel's airy interior made possible the twin helical staircase inside, which Bartholdi intended only for workmen. These stairs would later allow millions of visitors to climb to the Statue's head and look out from the windows in her crown.

Bartholdi (lower right) supervising wood and plaster model of Liberty's left arm.

a dollar. Money in hand, the pedestal was completed and workers began to reassemble the Statue on its final home.

Finally, on a cold, foggy October 28, 1886, Bartholdi unveiled his master work and President Grover Cleveland commended the monument to the ages. She was called *The Statue of Liberty Enlightening the World* and was understood to be gazing across the Atlantic, a symbol of French-American solidarity.

In 1892, an immigration center opened on nearby Ellis Island under the newly formed U.S. Immigration Bureau. During the years from 1892 to 1954, over 16 million immigrants were admitted to the United States through Ellis Island — the greatest mass migration of people in modern history. Because of its proximity to Ellis Island, the Statue of Liberty took on a new meaning as the "Mother of Exiles" for those who fled oppression in other lands. For many immigrants, the Statue was the first sight of America after a long and miserable journey by sea, encouraging them to invest their bravest hopes in the promise of freedom which the Statue proclaimed.

In a fund-raising exhibition for the pedestal, Emma Lazarus, a Sephardic Jew, had written a sonnet in which she emphasized the symbolic interpretation of the Statue. It was not until the massive immigration through New York Harbor began to peak that the message of her poem was fully understood. In 1903, two decades after it was written, the sonnet was inscribed on a plaque and placed inside the Statue's pedestal. Since only the concluding lines of the sonnet are well-known, it is worth quoting "The New Colossus" in its entirety:

Not like the brazen giant of Greek fame,
With conquering limbs astride from land to land;
Here at our sea-washed, sunset gates shall stand
A mighty woman with a torch, whose flame
Is the imprisoned lightning, and her name
Mother of Exiles. From her beacon-hand
Glows world-wide welcome; her mild eyes command
The air-bridged harbor that twin cities frame.
"Keep ancient lands, your storied pomp!" cries she
With silent lips. "Give me your tired, your poor,
Your huddled masses yearning to breathe free,
The wretched refuse of your teeming shore.
Send these, the homeless, tempest-tost to me,
I lift my lamp beside the golden door!"

During World War I, the Statue gained an added symbolic meaning, as ships bearing American troops steamed out of New York Harbor bound for European battlefields. Now Liberty began to signify the hope of America to "make the world safe for democracy."

Thus the Statue came to represent America itself. For decades the United States had had other such popular images — Yankee Doodle, Uncle Sam, and the eagle. Eventually the Statue surpassed all of them as the quintessential symbol of America.

Political cartoonists could be sure of being understood when they portrayed the Lady with the torch weeping, or hunched in senility, or holding her nose as the "Dregs of Europe" clustered at her feet. She also lent her fame to a wave of "commercialization," as the Statue began to appear in ads for Liberty bonds, then for products like pocket watches, cookie tins, chewing tobacco, and cleanser. Her folklore even extended to the movies — in the closing scene of *Planet of the Apes,* she appears buried to the chest in sand on an apocalyptic seashore.

The brilliance of Bartholdi, Eiffel, and scores of anonymous workmen had ensured that the Statue took its permanent place in the American mind. As the 1980's opened, a few people had begun to notice the ravages that a century's exposure to the elements had wreaked upon the great monument.

Liberty's torch on display at the 1876 U.S. Centennial Exhibition in Philadelphia.

13

October 28, 1886 Dedication Day of the Statue of Liberty.

Since 1933, the National Park Service has been the custodian of Liberty Island. Here, Superintendent David Moffitt helps to clear snow.

National Park Service Ranger with Liberty Island guard dog Tali.

Reconstruction

In May 1980, Ed Drummond, an eccentric but skilled rock climber from Britain, startled New York City by carrying out an unauthorized ascent of the Statue of Liberty. As thousands watched, some exhorting Drummond to fall and break his neck, the climber unfurled a political protest banner and made his slow and dangerous climb to a point between Liberty's shoulder blades. The chief ranger for the monument was outraged, assuming Drummond was hammering pitons (metal spikes) into the fragile skin of the Statue. After bivouacking overnight on a fold in one of the Lady's copper robes, Drummond rappelled down and was arrested.

Oddly enough, the impact of Drummond's stunt was wholly beneficial. When workers went to examine the expected damage, they found that the alpinist, practicing modern "clean climbing" techniques, had done no harm to the Statue's skin. Nevertheless, a century of corrosion, weathering, pollution and almost two million visitors annually, had taken their toll and a major restoration was essential. The right arm that bears the torch had become worn, as it swayed in a century's winds, by a spike protruding from Liberty's crown. Indeed, many elements of Liberty's structure required repair — from her base to the top of her badly damaged torch.

With the assistance of a group of experts and engineers, including the National Park Service's own preservation specialists, recommendations and plans for an extensive restoration were formed. The timing could not have been better. Every inch of the monument was scrutinized, inside and out, and in 1982, a massive renovation was launched. Its goal was to finish in time for a grand national celebration of the Statue, planned for the July 4th weekend of her centennial in 1986.

It was obvious that such a restoration would require vastly greater sums of money than the $400,000 it had cost to build the Statue in the 19th century. Just as President Ulysses S. Grant had done when the original proposal had been brought to him, so President Ronald W. Reagan decided that the Statue's restoration, along with that of Ellis Island, should be funded not by government, but by contributions from individual citizens, private organizations, and corporations. In May 1982, the Secretary of the Interior appointed Lee A. Iacocca, whose parents had come from Italy to America through the gates of Ellis Island, to head The Statue of Liberty-Ellis Island Centennial Commission. The Commission was established as an advisory group to the Interior Department and the National Park Service on all matters pertaining to the

restoration. Later, Lee Iacocca became Chairman of The Statue of Liberty-Ellis Island Foundation, Inc., a private non-profit organization charged with fundraising, restoration management and centennial celebrations planning. The initial estimated cost of restoring the Statue and Ellis Island was $230 million, later increased to $265 million as the restoration plans for Ellis Island were amended.

As workers began the unprecedented overhaul, it was hoped that the Statue would remain open for visitors. It soon became obvious, however, that conditions were too hectic and hazardous for the public. The Statue was closed to visitors for two years beginning in April 1984. Never before had the monument been closed for so long.

Just as the original builders achieved brilliant feats of construction, so did the restorers. The most visible was a gigantic free-standing scaffolding, the largest ever erected. Six thousand pieces of aluminum were laboriously put together to make a 26-story cocoon around the Statue. Incredibly, the scaffolding never touched the delicate copper skin of the Lady, giving it a berth everywhere of 18 inches to allow for swaying in the wind. The scaffolding was so well constructed it survived Hurricane Gloria intact.

Not surprisingly, morale on the construction crew was extremely high. The first workers up the scaffolding kissed the Lady. "It was the job of the century," said a vice-president for the supervising construction firm.

Much of the outer skin was found to be in basically good shape, but a number of pieces of the original copper sheeting had to be replaced. Molds were made of damaged areas, holes were patched and sealed, and the whole skin was given a thorough wash. Inside, matters were more problematic. The protective asbestos pads which Bartholdi had inserted between copper skin and iron armature bars had crumbled away, causing the iron to come in contact with the copper and deteriorate from electrolytic corrosion. It became clear that nearly all the 1800 bars would have to be replaced. Since these crucial links were what held the skin to the skeleton inside, only a few at a time could be changed. Moreover, each stainless-steel replacement had to be shaped exactly to match the iron original, and no two of Bartholdi's 1800 bars were alike. At their most efficient pace, the laborers could replace only 70 bars a week.

Another demanding task was cleaning the interior of the skin of seven coats of paint and two of coal tar. Everything from sand to glass beads to walnut shells to corn cobs was tried, until finally a combination of liquid nitrogen for the paint and plain old baking soda for the tar did do the job. Many of the renovations were aimed at making the interior more comfortable and attractive for visitors. A new hydraulic lift replaced the old elevator; new ventilation systems were designed to curb the wild extremes of temperature inside; and the plumbing and electrical systems were overhauled. Most importantly, the wire mesh walls surrounding the staircase were taken down, allowing visitors to appreciate, for the first time, the dramatic interior space of the monument.

The only part of the Statue that had to be completely replaced was the upper half of the torch, which had already undergone many facelifts and redesigns. In 1916 Gutzon Borglum, the sculptor of Mt. Rushmore, redesigned the torch with leaded-style panes of glass to improve its working as the lighthouse it was intended to be. During the restoration the old torch was removed in one piece by a crane and used as a model for the new torch. A group of French artisans skilled at *repoussé*, an ancient method of shaping metal into patterns in relief by hammering the reverse side into molds, won the commission to construct the new torch. Repoussé was the technique originally used to construct the Statue. The design — an opaque flame gilded with 24-karat gold leaf — actually returns to a design close to Bartholdi's original plan.

Dramatically illustrated above is the irreversible damage to the torch.

A new museum on the history and symbolism of the Statue is one the most popular features of the renovated monument. The lawns, walkways, plazas, and piers surrounding the Statue have been thoroughly relandscaped. After an early look at the restoration, architectural critic Paul Goldberger of *The New York Times* called it "an extraordinary event." In coming years, millions of visitors will concur.

Given the unprecedented fund-raising goal of $265 million, the Foundation sought the help of corporate America. The Foundation offered the use of its copyrighted and trademarked logo to "Official Sponsors" for marketing purposes. Major corporations pledged millions in the first year alone. But just as Joseph Pulitzer had done a century ago, the Foundation sought the support of individual citizens. As a result of these efforts, Lee Iacocca announced at the Liberty Weekend 1986 celebration that the Foundation had passed its goal.

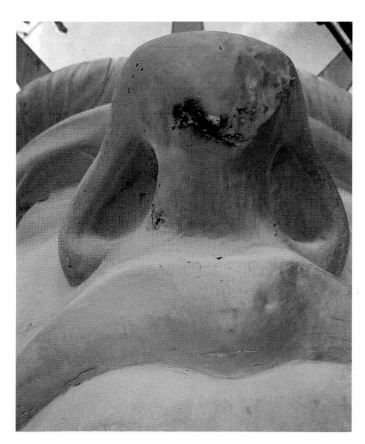

Damage to Liberty's skin can be seen in the nose.

17

Scaffolding arrives on Liberty Island in January 1984.

The National Park Service maintains the grounds even during the restoration.

Inspecting old armature bars prior to display in new museum.

Workers begin the access ramp to the scaffolding in February 1984.

Outer layer of scaffolding nearing completion.

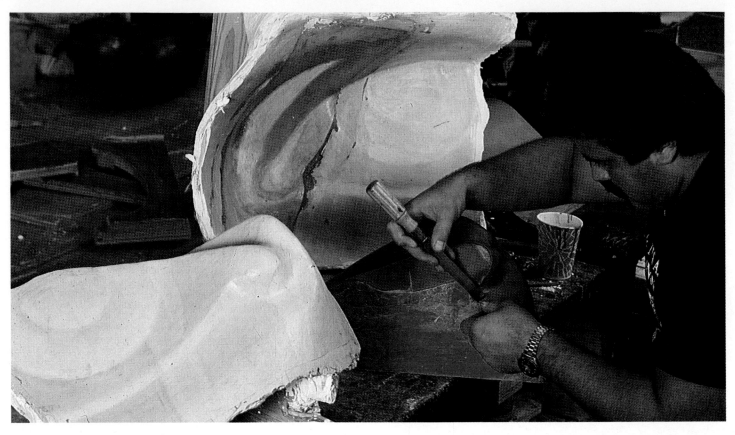

Worker making polymer mold for repair of eye.

Using a special non-toxic material Vanessa H. Hohaeb makes impression of Liberty's nose.

Richard Knoor finalizes a mold before metal work begins.

Damaged areas of nose were removed.

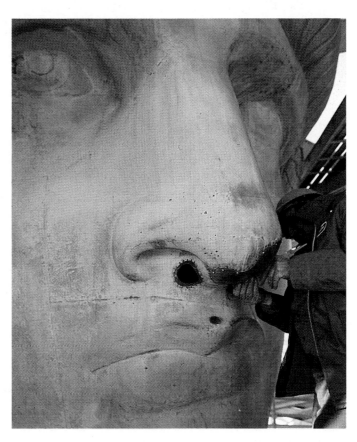

New copper sections are fitted into place.

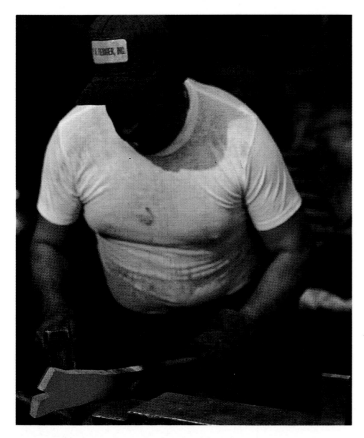

Worker making new armature bar using non-corrosive stainless steel.

An ironworker replaces one of the 1800 armature bars.

French and American workers remove a damaged spike from Liberty's crown for repair.

Repaired spike being fitted into place.

To create the new flame, an architect compares a clay model to the old flame.

Workers preparing old flame for removal.

The old flame is carefully lowered to the ground, July 4, 1984

Annealing the copper for the new flame in preparation for shaping.

Making the final touches to the new balcony railing of the torch.

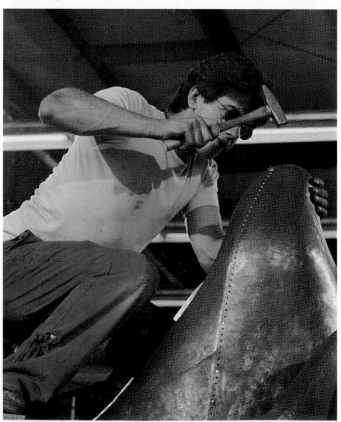

Riveting the tip of the new flame into place.

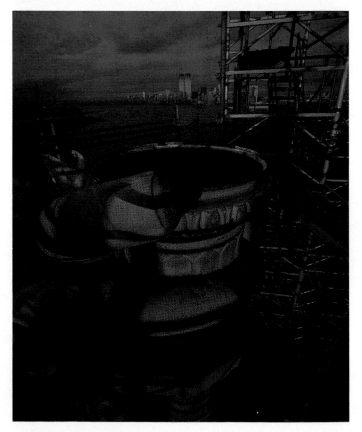

Empty torch awaiting arrival of new flame.

24

French and American artisans posed proudly with the newly finished flame.

Sample piece of copper showing the many steps required for gold leafing.

Robert and Fabrice Gohard, a father and son team, gold leaf the new flame.

Fifteen ounces of 24 karat gold was used to gild the new flame.

The new flame begins its ascent to the torch...

...and is fitted into place.

Towards the end of the restoration, the scaffolding comes down...

...stains on the Statue's base are removed...

...new steps at the base are installed...

...and the landscaping chores are finished up.

Preparations

As the planning for Liberty Weekend 1986 gathered momentum, it became evident that the scale of the celebration itself would have to be monumental. Bartholdi had once said, "Colossal statuary is not just a matter of thinking big. It should touch the spectator's feelings, not by reason of its sheer size, but because its size is right for the idea that prompted it." His words might equally apply to the national celebration that would climax the long restoration of the Statue of Liberty.

The man in charge of Liberty Weekend was David L. Wolper, who had impeccable credentials for organizing events on a grand scale. It was Wolper who had programmed the spectacular opening and closing ceremonies of the 1984 Olympics; he had also produced the successful and engrossing TV mini-series *Roots*. In every event, Mr. Wolper proved himself to be up to the task of organizing the greatest celebration this nation has ever seen.

It was argued that no event of this magnitude had ever been planned, and the size of the potential problems was proportional to the scale of the party. No one could predict how many tourists would descend on New York City. Informed estimates ranged from 5 to 13 million. From the start, New York's Mayor Ed Koch participated enthusiastically in the planning. The logistics required bold steps. Lower Manhattan, south of Chambers Street, would become an auto-free zone at 7:00 P.M. on the first day, remaining so until mid-

night on the last. The effect would be to turn the oldest part of the city into a wall-to-wall street fair. Every bus and subway train the city owned would be called into service, and lines would run on continuous peak rush-hour schedules. Parks in Queens and Staten Island would be given over to camping and recreational vehicles. To insure pleasant and safe conditions, the city would spend some $6 million on overtime and temporary help alone.

Though hundreds of different events were scheduled, the extravaganza was built around several spectacular high points. These included a swearing-in ceremony on Ellis Island of nearly 300 new citizens by Warren E. Burger, Chief Justice of the United States; a dramatic relighting of the torch by President Reagan; a parade of ships including 21 Class A Tall Ships, modeled after the centerpiece of the 1976 Bicentennial; the largest fireworks display America had ever seen; and a glittering closing ceremony at The Meadowlands in nearby New Jersey. The indomitable Wolper promised the country a "50-goose-bump event" — and it was.

An idea of the grand scale of preparations can be gained from the incredible logistics required for the Tall Ships and fireworks display. The organizational planning to arrange safe control and passage through and around New York Harbor was staggering. The parade of ships included 250 historic sailing vessels featuring 21 magnificent Tall Ships which travelled long and, for many, hazardous voyages to pay tribute to the Lady.

Accommodations, such as food, entertainment, and in some cases, English interpreters for the captains and crews of these ships, had to be arranged. Similar provisions had to be made for the captains and crews of the 30 naval vessels that came from all over the world.

In addition, arrangements for a projected 30,000 plus private spectator boats, ranging in size from a one-person kayak, to enormous pleasure yachts, had to be planned. The Operation Sail 1986 committee accepted the challenge of handling these requirements, even to the extent of providing 25,000 cheeseburgers for the crews of the Tall Ships. The U.S. Coast Guard accepted the responsibility and competently provided safe passage, control and anchorages in the tricky harbor currents for all these vessels.

The fireworks display, lasting for almost half an hour, consisted of 40,000 projectiles fired from 41 barges placed into predetermined positions by expert tugboat operators. Six hundred thousand pounds of mortars connected by 60 miles of wire, all centrally controlled by computer, were used to set up the display. From tugboat operators to top-level pyrotechnicians, hundreds of personnel enthusiastically worked to-

The old New York Customs House prepares for the celebration.

gether to arrange the most spectacular fireworks extravaganza this nation has ever seen. As a result of these grand scale preparations, there were no major injuries or incidents reported.

Perhaps the most nerve-rattling of the planners' headaches was security, for the celebration struck more than one observer as a prime target for terrorists. To guard against any number of possible scenarios, the FBI coordinated the efforts of five agencies — the Secret Service, the U.S. Navy, the U.S. Coast Guard, the National Park Service, and the New York City Police. However, no agency could guarantee good weather. A wet, rainy day like the one experienced at the Statue's unveiling in 1886 could be a major disappointment, and fog over the harbor, with thousands of ships on the loose, could lead to disaster.

As the weekend neared, everyone seemed to be taking the difficulties in stride and looking forward to four glorious days of fun. The special New York wit came to the fore, as in a remark by Rabbi Haskel Lookstein. In response to an appeal by Cardinal John O'Connor that bells in all the country's churches be rung for 100 seconds on July 3, the rabbi said he would be glad to help. Since synagogues do not have bells, as Lookstein pointed out, he would contribute by sounding the burglar alarm.

Posing for their pictures with cut-outs of President Reagan was popular with the crowds.

Statue of Liberty crowns were fast-selling souvenirs.

Shop windows and storefronts all over New York were decorated for the coming festivities.

July 3, 1986
Ceremony

On the eve of Liberty Weekend, Executive Producer David Wolper's greatest fear was of rain — "the one thing," he wrote in a diary kept for USA Today, *"I couldn't do anything about." High winds on the night of July 2 did in fact keep some of the massive fleet of ships from entering New York Harbor, but July 3, though cool and windy, stayed blessedly dry.*

By early morning huge crowds had gathered in lower Manhattan to touch off the celebration. The street vendors did a brisk business. Among the favorite souvenirs were foam rubber crowns shaped like the Statue's — in green, pink, and of course, red, white, and blue. Liberty headgear had become so voguish that a makeup artist named Mark Traynor was selling $1500 "Freedom Wigs" that turned women into walking replicas of the copper-plated lady. On the streets, hawkers sold tourists their own picture next to cardboard cutouts of President Reagan, Miss Liberty, "Miami Vice" star Don Johnson, and Mets pitcher Dwight Gooden. Hot dogs and beer were consumed in gargantuan quantities, and one ice cream stand put up a sign announcing a special "express lane: vanilla only."

Throughout most of the day, the main attraction was the gathering of ships in the harbor. The fleet of U.S. Navy warships made a dramatic entry under the Verrazano Narrows Bridge. T.V. broadcasts, live from huge blimps, gave a spectacular view of the steady influx of boats large and small. Some news journalists resorted to unusual ways of transmitting information — like the photographers who sent their exposed film in by carrier pigeon.

From ringside on the Battery waterfront, the sailors on the aircraft carriers looked like miniature figures lined up in white uniforms. Even the docked tugboats became things of beauty. A few intrepid kayakers darted in and out among the bulky ships, earning the admiration of the crowd. There was speculation among the spectators about terrorism, but one man offered a reassuring view: "If our warships can detect missiles in the Atlantic, I think they can do the same in the Hudson." There was a surprising number of French tourists in the crowd — some happily arm-in-arm, singing the *"Marseillaise."*

Uptown, a gathering of 3000 people, including Bob Hope and Helen Hayes, attended a two-hour mass at St. Patrick's Cathedral. As night fell on Ellis Island, Chief Justice Warren Burger swore in 270 new U.S. citizens, including ballet star Mikhail Baryshnikov, who was then quickly transported across the harbor to take part in the Opening Ceremonies

The press struggled for good viewing position during the weekend.

— dancing for the first time as a U.S. citizen. The outdoor swearing-in ceremony was conducted with the formal pomp of a courtroom proceeding, coordinated to the second with similar proceedings in 44 cities around the country. The new citizens stood, hands raised in oath, and solemnly repeated the pledge after Chief Justice Burger:

I hereby declare, on oath, / that I renounce all allegiance and fidelity / to any foreign prince or potentate, / state or sovereignty, / of which I have heretofore been / a subject or citizen; / that I will support and defend / the Constitution and laws / of the United States of America / against all enemies, foreign and domestic; / that I will bear true faith / and allegiance to the same; / that I will bear arms on behalf of the United States / when required by law; / that I will perform noncombatant service / in the Armed Forces of the United States / when required by law; / that I will perform work of national importance / under civilian direction / when required by law / and that I take this obligation freely / without any mental reservation / or purpose of evasion; / so help me God.

On Governors Island, a VIP crowd of 3,000 sat in bleachers captivated by a galaxy of stars. Breathtaking performances were given by Neil Diamond, Shirley MacLaine, Jose Feliciano, Kenny Rogers, Andy Williams and Frank Sinatra in an open-air theatre.

David Wolper led the formalities preceding the official unveiling of the Statue by declaring, "During the course of the next few days, we will try to impart some of the profound and pleasant meaning this Statue has for countless Americans and freedom-loving people everywhere." Lee Iacocca announced to a cheering crowd that the Foundation had met and exceeded its fund-raising goal.

President and Mrs. Reagan along with President and Mrs. Mitterrand of France paid tribute to the long friendship between their two countries. In addition, President Reagan praised the spirit of the workers who had labored on the restoration of Miss Liberty. President Reagan quoted a young Harry Truman who described the Statue in a letter to his wife: "I've never seen anything that looked so good." The President added, "It is good to know that Miss Liberty is still giving life to the dream of a new world where old antagonisms could be cast aside and people of every nation could live together as one." Then the President pushed a button, and a laser beam suddenly illuminated the pedestal of the Statue in red light. As the laser swept upwards, it changed to blue, then finally to the white light of fifteen 6,000 watt lamps, which emblazoned the Lady in splendor.

During the ceremonies that followed, the President presented Medals of Liberty to 12 distinguished naturalized Americans: Irving Berlin, Franklin R. Chang-Diaz, Kenneth Clark, Hanna Holborn Gray, Bob Hope, Henry A. Kissinger, I.M. Pei, Itzhak Perlman, James B. Reston, Albert Sabin, An Wang, and Elie Wiesel. Finally, as the Statue was once more eclipsed in darkness, it came time for the relighting of the torch. Without being bidden, the VIP guests on Governors Island spontaneously rose to their feet. Abruptly, a laser beam isolated the arm and the torch. People gasped involuntarily, and the band burst into John Philip Sousa's "Stars and Stripes Forever."

(Right and Below): Five huge blimps raced around the Statue delighting the crowds.

The aircraft carrier John F. Kennedy arrives and takes her position in the harbor.

Young Kenneth Mack, Jr. performs the "Star Spangled Banner" at the Opening Ceremonies.

President Mitterrand of France addresses the guests and the nation.

Chief Justice Warren Burger (third from right) prior to the swearing-in of new citizens on Ellis Island.

Gladness and pride are reflected in the faces of the new citizens.

The new Americans stand to recite the oath of citizenship.

The stage of the Opening Ceremonies is aglow at dusk.

Lee A. Iacocca delivers his opening remarks on Governors Island.

President Reagan delivers his opening remarks to launch Liberty Weekend.

With wife Nancy by his side, President Reagan pays tribute to our friendship with France and to the workers on the restoration project.

At the completion of the President's speech, a laser beam dramatically strikes the base of the Statue...

the Statue of Liberty is slowly illuminated in brilliant light...

...until the Lady is gloriously aglow.

Neil Diamond continues the evening's entertainment with the Immigrant Pageant.

The Medal of Liberty awards are presented to twelve distinguished naturalized Americans.

Mikhail Baryshnikov, sworn in as an American citizen only minutes before, dances in performance with Leslie Browne...

...and receives the applause of the crowd.

Beautiful Elizabeth Taylor moderated a portion of the evening.

At President Reagan's signal, the torch of Liberty is relighted bringing the evening toward its dramatic close.

July 4, 1986
Tradition

July 4th has always been a day of festivities in America culminating in many small towns across the country in an evening fireworks display. Liberty Weekend's July 4th fit this pattern . . . but on a much grander scale. Of the four days devoted to commemorating the Statue of Liberty's hundredth birthday, the Fourth was the most purely celebratory — in the words of President Reagan, "the most fun."

July 4th was a perfect day, with brilliant sun, little wind, and temperatures in the 80s. The day was devoted almost entirely to three events: the breathtaking parade of ships and flybys of planes, the Harbor Festival that turned lower Manhattan into a gigantic street fair, and the largest fireworks show ever seen in the United States.

From the huge crowds of July 3, the throng swelled steadily on the Fourth as subways disgorged one trainload after another of spectators. As one journalist described it, "New York looked as if some giant hand had dumped the island on its end and shaken everybody down to the southern tip." Along with the vendors selling hot dogs and day-glo T-shirts, a troupe of street performers took advantage of the largest captive audience they would ever find. An organist at Trinity Church in the heart of the financial district played many favorite tunes, with "My Country

'Tis of Thee" rousing the crowd to patriotic fervor. A juggler on South Street tossed an apple, a torch, and a cleaver directly above a reclining woman, as he hyped the crowd: "Your applause will save this woman!" There were ethnic dances of every sort. At McSorley's Saloon, the oldest pub in New York, the owner proudly invited beer-drinkers to take a look at an original 1883 poster of the Statue of Liberty.

The parade of ships began with the International Naval Review. President Reagan and French President Francois Mitterrand boarded the USS Iowa, and conducted the review of warships from all over the world. In remarks prior to the beginning of the review, President Reagan commented, "It's been said that we Americans count our blessings too seldom — but not this weekend. This weekend we celebrate, my friends, we cut loose." And cut loose we did. An estimated 30,000 pleasure boats of all sizes packed the harbor, an unprecedented throng. An estimated two million spectators lined the shore, attempting to catch a glimpse of the stately procession. In Battery Park the crowd was immense, with children struggling to see the Lady they had come to honor.

Above the harbor, crack flight teams from France, Britain, and the United States, including the famous U.S. Navy Blue Angels and the U.S. Airforce Thunderbirds, streaked across the sky. Skywriting aircraft

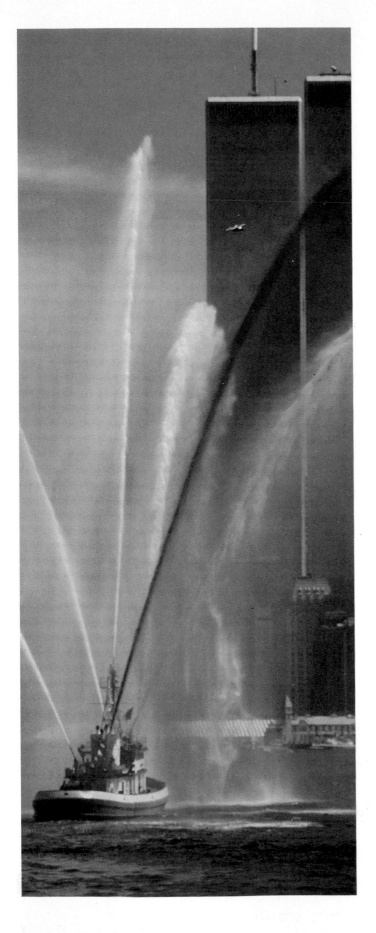

blazoned, "U.S. Navy Salutes Ships of the World," and an assemblage of blimps meandered through the blue sky. Pleasure boats jockeyed for viewing position, and Mayor Edward Koch cruised by in a police boat with siren wailing and waved ebulliently to the crowd.

At last the Tall Ships began their stately promenade. This time twice as many ships participated in Operation Sail 1986 than in OpSail 1976. The largest ship in the parade was the 345 foot long *Libertad* from Argentina, and the oldest was Philadelphia's *Gazela,* built in 1883. As the parade began, David Wolper, ever the perfectionist, worried that the USS Eagle, the U.S. Coast Guard's Tall Ship which would lead the procession, would arrive before the President could officially start the parade. At the last minute, the Eagle slowed down and the timing came off perfectly.

In the evening, the Boston Pops gave a splendid and varied concert — nationally televised — from Liberty State Park in New Jersey. It was the first time in 102 years that the Boston Pops Orchestra was absent from Boston on the 4th of July. A fanfare composed by conductor John Williams opened the concert in bravura fashion, as the Pops brass were supplemented by 120 additional trumpeters. Popular performers representing a variety of entertainment styles sang and danced for Lady Liberty.

President Reagan launched the gala fireworks show by telling the nation, "My fellow Americans, we are known around the world as a confident and happy people. Tonight there is much to celebrate and many blessings to be grateful for. So while it's good to talk about serious things, it is just as important and just as American to have some fun. Now — let the celebration begin."

Three minutes before the first rocket exploded, Tommy Walker — whom David Wolper regards as our country's foremost fireworks expert — called Wolper to tell him everything was in order. Fireworks are as hard to describe in cold prose as the ineffable beauty of music. The cheering of the crowd could be heard resounding across the harbor between detonations. Americans had never before seen such a spectacular 4th of July fireworks display.

Children, as well as adults, were caught up in the spirit of Liberty Weekend.

Young members of the crew of the Norwegian Tall Ship *Christian Radich* take in the sights of New York.

Balloons, T-shirts, Liberty crowns and homemade costumes added to the color of the festivities.

The U.S. Coast Guard had the monumental task of controlling traffic in New York Harbor.

30,000 ships and boats jockeyed for good viewing position in the harbor.

President Reagan arrives aboard the battleship Iowa to begin the Naval Review.

Fireboats add their own salute during the Naval Review.

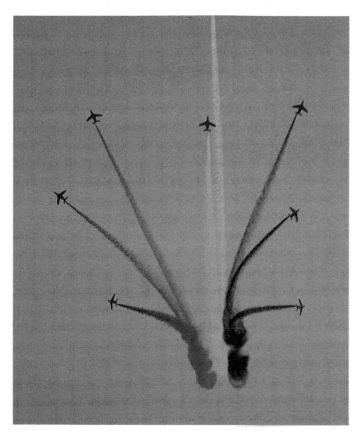

Precision flying teams performed colorful "flyovers" throughout the day.

A Japanese warship passes in review.

Seen from atop the Verrazano Narrows Bridge, a Tall Ship sails toward the harbor.

The USS Eagle, the U.S. Coast Guard's Tall Ship, leads the magnificent parade of sail.

The parade of ships passes closely by the USS Iowa.

A panoramic view of ships and skyline as seen from the enormous deck of the aircraft carrier John F. Kennedy.

Sailors stand on the yard arms as they salute the Lady.

All along the shore crowds were awestruck by the stately beauty of the Tall Ships.

Smoke trails across the harbor as ships fire guns and cannon in salute.

Seamen dot the rigging of a Class A Tall Ship.

The Italian Tall Ship Amerigo Vespucci represents her country in the Salute to the Statue of Liberty.

With the Verrazano Narrows Bridge in the background, the Irish J-Boat and a Tall Ship take their places in the parade.

New York's mayor Ed Koch was an enthusiastic spectator.

Liberty Weekend Chairman David L. Wolper wears a cap presented to him by the crew of the John F. Kennedy.

Old fashioned 4th of July picnics were the order of the day.

Liberty sunglasses were a popular souvenir item.

In anticipation of the fireworks, crowds began to form during the afternoon.

A young woman wears one of the more elaborate costumes seen during Liberty Weekend.

65

Special parking areas were established for the thousands of spectators with campers and recreational vehicles.

Omar K. Lerman (at head of table), field commander of the fireworks display, leads a coordination meeting prior to the big event.

A crane operator loads one of the huge barges used to launch the fireworks.

Mortars are set into position around the base of the Statue.

Inside the master control booth for the fireworks, the "script" for the evening sits upon the computer.

As evening falls the countdown begins.

Skyscrapers, including the Empire State Building, show traditional red, white and blue 4th of July colors.

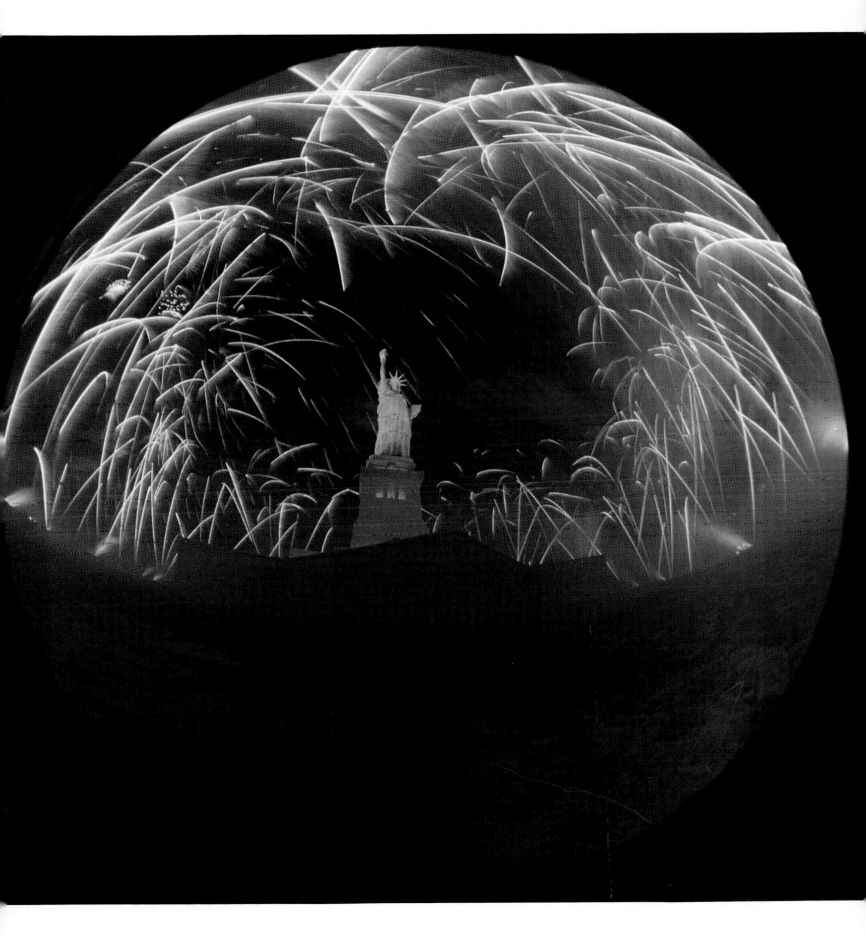

July 5, 1986
Culture

The main highlights of the third day of Liberty Weekend — Saturday, July 5th — were Nancy Reagan's official reopening of the Statue of Liberty to visitors and the free Central Park concert by the New York Philharmonic. Only 36 hours earlier it had been windy and chilly in New York Harbor. Now the weather had turned hot and humid, with temperatures climbing into the 90s.

It had been David Wolper's idea to center the reopening ceremony on children — partly, he half-joked, to "save me the headache of deciding which politicians are going to be first to enter the Statue of Liberty." The lucky children who participated in the reopening were winners of a nationwide essay contest. This contest was announced by David Wolper in his old school in New York, the day after the space shuttle Challenger disaster. During that announcement Wolper spontaneously named the competition for teacher/astronaut Christa McAuliffe. The reopening ceremony was as simple as the previous night's fireworks had been lavish. As doves of peace flew up into the sky, Mrs. Reagan cut a red, white, and blue ribbon. She then ascended to the crown of the Statue with two of the children, one from France and one from Alaska. Said

11-year-old Audrey Weir, from the Alsace region in France, "Oh, what a very sweet giant."

In her remarks, Mrs. Reagan cited a parallel between today and the 1880's, when schoolchildren had sent in pennies to help raise money for the Statue's pedestal. In the recent fund-raising effort, she noted, schools had raised $5 million for the restoration of the Statue. Then a group of French and American children began singing "Happy Birthday." Assuming they were saluting the Statue, Mrs. Reagan blushed when she realized that the youngsters were in fact congratulating her on her 65th birthday, which happened to be the very next day.

The urge to be among the first to enter the Statue had been so strong that some tourists had tried to line up on the evening of July 3, only to be dispersed by police. As it was, by the morning of the Fifth, a line of 4,000 people wound through Battery Park, as eager visitors queued up for the noon ferry to Liberty Island. The first ordinary tourist to step on Liberty Island was a British factory worker named Paul Weisman. He had camped out overnight in a sleeping bag on the pier.

The question being asked around Battery Park was, "Where do I get tickets to see the Statue?" Officers on duty quickly learned not to wait for the question, but to repeat the answer every time someone came near. There was dismay in the crowd as the rumor spread that once on the island, one had to wait five more hours to get inside the Statue.

Yet once they arrived, the visitors seemed not only patient but awestruck. Many carried long-stemmed roses to place inside the crown or at the Statue's base. And many spoke spontaneously to nearby strangers about their own parents' or grandparents' experience as immigrants.

Meanwhile, Harbor Festival continued with exciting events. One of the unusual events was a lifeboat race. Sue Lyons, rowing a one-ton lifeboat single-handedly, said, "You have to get yourself psyched up for this. It's like trying to row a bathtub across the harbor." In the air, five giant blimps raced 12 miles down the Hudson from the George Washington Bridge to the Statue.

Wolper dropped in on the rehearsal for the Sports Salute and the star-spangled Closing Ceremonies on Sunday. He found directors in a frenzy over technical problems, and even such accomplished performers as skaters Peggy Fleming and Dorothy Hamill apprehensive about performing before such a huge gathering. Yet Wolper started to relax. "Finally after six months of work I am beginning to feel good," he wrote in his diary. "I have a feeling we are on the way."

Some people had also been waiting all day in Central Park, where the New York Philharmonic, under the direction of Zubin Mehta, was to star in an evening gala of classical music. The struggle for seating space was intense, and for good reason, as attendance reached an estimated 800,000, making this the largest live classical music audience in history.

Hosting the concert were Kirk Douglas and Angela Lansbury. The music alternated between French and American compositions; an all-star cast of performers included singers Placido Domingo, Marilyn Horne, Leona Mitchell, Sherrill Milnes, violinist Itzhak Perlman, cellist Yo-Yo Ma, and conductor Zubin Mehta. The appropriate climax of the program was the "Ode to Joy," the fourth movement of Beethoven's beautiful Ninth Symphony described as "One of music's ultimate statements about the universal brotherhood of man."

Spectators use programs to provide shade on a very warm July 5.

On Liberty Island, the red carpet is rolled out for First Lady Nancy Reagan.

At the podium, Nancy Reagan receives a bouquet from a French schoolchild.

Christa McAuliffe essay contest winner, Jason Michael Verhelst, is honored at the Reopening Ceremony.

Lee Iacocca addresses the gathering and thanks America's youth for the important part they played in the restoration.

Assisted by one French and one American child, Mrs. Reagan cuts the ribbon and reopens the Statue of Liberty.

Secretary of the Interior, Donald Hodel, shakes the hand of the First Lady.

The Paris Boys Choir sang in tribute to the Lady.

Long lines of people wait to enter the restored Statue.

The old flame provides a centerpiece for the main lobby within the Statue's base.

The newly revamped staircase spiraling upward to Miss Liberty's crown.

Three generations of the Hill family have operated the Liberty Island concession stand.

Nancy Reagan waves from Liberty's crown.

Crowds gather for the International Concert on the Great Lawn in Central Park.

Under the direction of Zubin Mehta, the N.Y. Philharmonic provided music lovers with two hours of entertainment under the stars.

July 6, 1986 Celebration

By plan there was a wonderful symmetry about Liberty Weekend. The odd-numbered days — July 3 and 5 — were focused around relatively solemn, formal events: the swearing-in of our citizens, the relighting of the torch, the reopening of the Statue itself. And the even-numbered days — July 4 and 6 — were given over to fun and celebration. If the country's greatest fireworks show was the culminating event on the Fourth, the Closing Ceremonies in Giants Stadium at The Meadowlands on the evening of July 6th, ended the four-day celebration in a blaze of glorious entertainment.

At The Meadowlands in the Brendan Byrne Arena, some of the nation's best athletes participated in a Sports Salute to The Statue. Included among these legendary sports personalities were Henry Aaron, Rafer Johnson, Billie Jean King, Joe Namath, Mary Lou Retton, and Muhammad Ali, as well as dozens of other accomplished athletes. The huge crowd thrilled to the skills of Bart Conner on the parallel bars, the grace of Olympic medalist Peggy Fleming, and the grand finale in the center of the arena.

While clean-up crews performed herculean labors throughout Manhattan, a crowd of 47,500 assembled in The Meadowlands in New Jersey for the three-hour gala that closed the marathon weekend. Among the most dazzling of the spectacles was the opening drill team, composed of 850 high school girls who formed a giant Statue of Liberty on the playing field, then dissolved it into a waving American flag. Other stunning group performers included a 500-piece marching band playing the finale of "A Chorus Line."

The Closing Ceremonies were divided into three major parts: *Remember, Rejoice,* and *Renew.* Among the events of the *Remember* portion of the ceremonies was a Salute to France. Entertainer Kenny Rogers expressed America's appreciation for the generosity and friendship of the French people. Thirty-five riders and mounts of the Garde Républicaine Horse Guards paraded into the stadium wearing their traditional 19th Century military uniforms. Lee Iacocca thanked the many selfless individuals who worked to organize Liberty Weekend. As many of the men and women who helped to restore the Statue of Liberty took the stage, Mr. Iacocca presented a certificate to a representative member of their group.

Five time Grammy award winner Willie Nelson dedicated the song "Living in the Promiseland" to these workers. Then he performed with Kenny Rogers to conclude the *Remember* portion of the ceremonies.

Elizabeth Taylor introduced the *Rejoice* segment which featured the many forms of American music and entertainment. *Jazz* was performed by The Manhattan Transfer and Gerry Mulligan; *Rock and Roll* by The Temptations, The Four Tops, Bobby Rydell, and others. Then came *Country* music and the excited crowd witnessed several hundred banjo and fiddle players and 200 square dancers from all over the nation. Popular singer Waylon Jennings ended the *Country* portion.

At this point in the Closing Ceremonies, the audience of 65,000 was instructed by the announcer to find special flashlight lenses at their seats and to attach these lenses to the flashlights previously provided to them. The stadium was darkened and, on cue, the audience turned on the flashlights in a stirring display, spelling out LIBERTY around the huge arena.

Returning to the musical gala, the *Gospel* section featured a 250 voice choir joined by Billy Preston and Patti LaBelle as the stadium reverberated with the joyous strains of gospel music. Following *Gospel* came *Hollywood*. All the fantasy and glamour of the nation's movie industry was embodied by Shirley MacLaine in her elaborate dance number and by the legendary Gene Kelly with his stellar performance of "Singin' in the Rain."

In the *Contemporary* section, special effects wizardry flashed throughout the stadium as dancers joined the high-energy Pointer Sisters in a driving medley. Bringing us to the *Broadway* portion when 300 Liberty tap dancers clicked to the rhythms of a variety of Broadway tunes ending with Liza Minnelli's fabulous rendition of "New York, New York."

With the conclusion of the musical tribute to Liberty, Vice President George Bush addressed the audience and brought the events of Liberty Weekend to a poignant close, urging: "Tonight let us renew our devotion to the bright vision of America's future that the Statue of Liberty stands for." Cicely Tyson and Charlton Heston reflected upon America's future and the place of Liberty in American life. Then the Statue of Liberty All-American Marching Band struck up "America the Beautiful" — joined by the audience, who rose as one, to sing along as fireworks and lasers created a spectacular light show, bringing this nation's most fantastic party to an end.

From every aspect, Liberty Weekend was an astonishing success. All that was promised, happened — smoothly, and on time. Indeed, Liberty Weekend was even grander than expected. The patriotic spirit of the event infused the crowds and created a rare sense of celebration and brotherhood. None of the predicted catastrophes ever began to materialize. There was no terrorism, and the police made fewer arrests than at a football game. "Aqualock" failed to paralyze the parade of ships in New York Harbor, and the subway, bus, and train systems proved equal to the throngs who besieged lower Manhattan. There were no electronic glitches to interfere with the dramatic lighting and reopening of the Statue, and the tons of fireworks went off without causing any serious injuries. Even the weather played a supporting role.

Gymnast Cathy Rigby demonstrates the skills that made her an Olympic champion.

Captured by strobe photography, Bart Conner goes through his expert routine thrilling the crowd.

Final estimates of the number of people attending Liberty Weekend hovered around 6 million, one of the largest crowds in history. The Big Apple took in some $500 million in tourism revenue. It was estimated that over 500 million people around the world had watched at least part of ABC-TV's 17½ hours of coverage. Liberty Weekend was truly a series of big moments and once in a lifetime experiences.

In terms of its larger importance, Liberty Weekend, along with the dedicated restoration effort that preceded it, managed not only to renew the Statue of Liberty as one of the world's most famous monuments, but also to rekindle its symbolic meaning of freedom and liberty before a worldwide audience.

Of far greater significance in the long run was the spiritual and emotional impact of the celebration. If the 1976 Bicentennial did much to repair America's self-image after Vietnam and Watergate, Liberty Weekend put primary emphasis on the recognition of our nation as a unified people derived from vastly diversified ethnic origins. As President Reagan stated on July 4th, "The things that unite us — America's past of which we are so proud, our hopes and aspirations for the future of the world and this much loved country — these things far outweigh what little divides us."

Liberty Weekend was criticized by some as a commercial extravaganza, as a triumph of "show biz" over serious commemoration. Yet when the celebration was completed, it seemed, paradoxically enough, that the lavish party had carried itself through four action-packed days on a tide of morale and enthusiasm that no mere "show biz" hoopla could have generated. It was a genuine outpouring of popular feeling. As Samuel G. Freedman wrote in the *New York Times*, "Whatever the formal events proved to be — a spellbinding spectacle of fireworks and Tall Ships, and a triumph of logistics besides — the less calculated side of the holiday offered the most genuinely moving tableaux. When Liberty Weekend was most lighthearted, it was most profound."

Speaking of Liberty Weekend in a personal letter to David Wolper, President Reagan said, "There are no words to properly thank you for that magnificent birthday party. You took a great city, a vast harbor, several islands and made them into a stage on which you produced a show for an entire nation. And an entire nation's heart was touched."

Camera and sound crews make final preparations to their equipment in anticipation of the evening's events.

Hundreds of colorful balloons soared gracefully out of the stadium.

The Statue of Liberty All-American Marching Band created visual as well as musical entertainment.

Lee Iacocca and David Wolper thank the many people who made Liberty Weekend possible.

The Liberty Dance Corps and Drill Team dazzle the audience with their performance.

Men and women representing the restoration workers were presented a certificate of appreciation for their diligent and unfailing work.

Willie Nelson (center) dedicates the song "Living In The Promiseland" to the workers.

The 150 Liberty Dancers and the 850 Drill Team members created a living American flag.

Gerry Mulligan (right) and the Manhattan Transfer provide their special blend of jazz for the Rejoice portion of the Ceremonies.

The Temptations lend their distinctive sound to commemorate American Rock & Roll.

Flashing back to the 1950's, a whimsical note was provided by the Elvis Presley imitators.

Several hundred banjo and fiddle players launch a country, folk, and western music jamboree.

Waylon Jennings exhibits his remarkable talent when concluding the Country portion of the show.

Upon instructions from the announcer, the audience of 65,000 participated in a shimmering flashlight display in the darkened stadium.

The Hollywood production number epitomized all the fantasy and glamour of the silver screen.

Kenny Rogers acknowledges Americans of diverse cultural heritage, who helped make the restoration of the Statue possible.

102

During the Broadway section of the Ceremonies, the irresistible Liza Minnelli gave an extraordinary performance, concluding with "New York, New York."

Cicely Tyson and Charlton Heston, two of America's finest dramatic performers, reflect on the meaning of liberty.

The Statue of Liberty All-American Marching Band, joined by 850 members of the Drill Team, created a final surprise on the field...

...as they formed a map of the USA, the band played "America the Beautiful" to resounding applause.

Fireworks, lights and an incredible laser show provide a glorious finale to America's greatest party.

Bob Kearney, a worker on the restoration project, displays the award presented him by Lee Iacocca.

Picture Credits

Page

6: ©John Dominis/Wheeler Pictures, 1986
8: ©Peter B. Kaplan, 1986, photo by J. Stephen Hall
9: (lower left) ©Peter B. Kaplan, 1986, photo by Michael C. Radigan; (right) ©Peter B. Kaplan, 1986, photo by Eric S. Cohen
10: ©Peter B. Kaplan, 1986
12: Freelance Photographers Guild/Library of Congress
13: Freelance Photographers Guild/Library of Congress
14: (top) Freelance Photographers Guild/Library of Congress; (bottom) ©Peter B. Kaplan, 1986
16: ©Peter B. Kaplan, 1986
17: ©Peter B. Kaplan, 1986
18: ©Peter B. Kaplan, 1986
19: ©Peter B. Kaplan, 1986
20: ©Peter B. Kaplan, 1986
21: ©Peter B. Kaplan, 1986
22: ©Peter B. Kaplan, 1986
23: ©Peter B. Kaplan, 1986
24: ©Peter B. Kaplan, 1986
25: ©Peter B. Kaplan, 1986
26: ©Peter B. Kaplan, 1986
27: ©Peter B. Kaplan, 1986
28: ©Peter B. Kaplan, 1986
30: (upper right) ©Peter B. Kaplan, 1986; (lower left) ©Don Dempsey/White Light, 1986
31: ©Don Dempsey/White Light, 1986
32: ©Don Dempsey/White Light, 1986
33: ©Don Dempsey/White Light, 1986
36: ©Peter B. Kaplan, 1986, photo by J. Stephen Hall
37: ©Peter B. Kaplan, 1986
38: ©Andrew Popper, 1986, Peter B. Kaplan Images, Ltd.
39: ©Declan Haun, 1986, Peter B. Kaplan Images, Ltd.
40: (top and lower left) ©Barbara Baumann, 1986, Peter B. Kaplan Images, Ltd.; (lower right) ©Annie Griffiths, 1986, Peter B. Kaplan Images, Ltd.
41: ©Declan Haun, 1986, Peter B. Kaplan Images, Ltd.
42: (top) ©Andrew Popper, 1986, Peter B. Kaplan Images, Ltd.; (bottom) ©Caroline Sheen, 1986, Peter B. Kaplan Images, Ltd.
43: ©Peter B. Kaplan, 1986, photo by J. Stephen Hall
44: ©Peter B. Kaplan, 1986
45: ©Caroline Sheen, 1986, Peter B. Kaplan Images, Ltd.
46: (top) ©Declan Haun, 1986, Peter B. Kaplan Images, Ltd.; (bottom) ©Andrew Popper, 1986, Peter B. Kaplan Images, Ltd.
47: ©Peter B. Kaplan, 1986
50: ©Ellis Vener, 1986, Peter B. Kaplan Images, Ltd.
51: (top) ©Edward Freeman/White Light, 1986; (bottom) ©Don Dempsey/White Light, 1986
52: (left) ©Laura M. Mueller, 1986, Peter B. Kaplan Images, Ltd.; (right) ©Richard Carter, 1986
53: ©Peter B. Kaplan, 1986
54: (top) ©Barbara Baumann, 1986, Peter B. Kaplan Images, Ltd.; (bottom) ©Monica R. Cipnic, 1986, Peter B. Kaplan Images, Ltd.
55: (top left) ©Laura M. Mueller, 1986, Peter B. Kaplan Images, Ltd.; (lower left) ©Andrew Popper, 1986, Peter B. Kaplan Images, Ltd.; (right) ©Annie Griffiths, 1986, Peter B. Kaplan Images, Ltd.
56: ©Ellis Vener, 1986, Peter B. Kaplan Images, Ltd.
57: ©Annie Griffiths, 1986, Peter B. Kaplan Images, Ltd.
58: (top) ©Joel Gordon, 1986, Peter B. Kaplan Images, Ltd.; (bottom) ©Peter B. Kaplan, 1986
59: ©Peter B. Kaplan, 1986
60/61: ©Michael Newler, 1986, Peter B. Kaplan Images, Ltd.
62: (top) Barbara Baumann, 1986, Peter B. Kaplan Images, Ltd.; (bottom) ©Michael C. Radigan, 1986, Peter B. Kaplan Images, Ltd.

Page

63: (top) ©James R. Irving, 1986, Peter B. Kaplan Images, Ltd.; (bottom) ©Peter B. Kaplan, 1986
64: (top left) ©Caroline Sheen, 1986, Peter B. Kaplan Images, Ltd.; (top right and below) ©Declan Haun, 1986, Peter B. Kaplan Images, Ltd.
65: (top left) ©Steven Borns, 1986, Peter B. Kaplan Images, Ltd.; (lower left) ©Richard Carter, 1986; (right) ©Joel Gordon, 1986, Peter B. Kaplan Images, Ltd.
66: (top) ©Joel Gordon, 1986, Peter B. Kaplan Images, Ltd.; (bottom) ©Peter B. Kaplan, 1986
67: ©Peter B. Kaplan, 1986
68: ©Aziz Rahman, 1986, Peter B. Kaplan Images, Ltd.
69: ©Peter B. Kaplan, 1986
70: (top) ©Peter B. Kaplan, 1986; (bottom) ©Steven Borns, 1986, Peter B. Kaplan Images, Ltd.
71: ©Peter B. Kaplan, 1986
72: ©Peter B. Kaplan, 1986
73: (top) ©Peter B. Kaplan, 1986; (bottom) ©Aziz Rahman, 1986, Peter B. Kaplan Images, Ltd.
74/75: ©Laura M. Mueller, 1986, Peter B. Kaplan Images, Ltd.
76/77: ©Aziz Rahman, 1986, Peter B. Kaplan Images, Ltd.
78: ©Shawn Michael, 1986, Peter B. Kaplan Images, Ltd.
80: ©Peter B. Kaplan, 1986
81: (top) ©The White House; (bottom) ©Tannenbaum/Sygma
82: ©Tannenbaum/Sygma
83: ©Peter B. Kaplan, 1986
84: ©Peter B. Kaplan, 1986
85: ©Peter B. Kaplan, 1986
86: ©Walker/Gamma-Liaison
87: (top) ©Peter B. Kaplan, 1986, photo by J. Stephen Hall; (bottom) Barbara Baumann, 1986, Peter B. Kaplan Images, Ltd.
90: ©Caroline Sheen, 1986, Peter B. Kaplan Images, Ltd.
91: ©Declan Haun, 1986, Peter B. Kaplan Images, Ltd.
92: ©Peter B. Kaplan, 1986, photo by Susan B. Cummings
93: ©Peter B. Kaplan, 1986
94: ©Peter B. Kaplan, 1986
95: (top) ©Peter B. Kaplan, 1986; (bottom) ©Peter B. Kaplan, 1986, photo by Eric S. Cohen
96: (top) ©Peter B. Kaplan, 1986; (bottom) ©Peter B. Kaplan, 1986, photo by J. Stephen Hall
97: (top) ©Peter B. Kaplan, 1986, photo by Susan B. Cummings; (bottom) ©Peter B. Kaplan, 1986
98: ©Peter B. Kaplan, 1986, photo by Eric S. Cohen
99: (top) ©Peter B. Kaplan, 1986, photo by J. Stephen Hall; (bottom) Barbara Baumann, 1986, Peter B. Kaplan Images, Ltd.
100: (top) Barbara Baumann, 1986, Peter B. Kaplan Images, Ltd.; (lower left) ©Peter B. Kaplan, 1986; (lower right) ©Peter B. Kaplan, 1986, photo by Susan B. Cummings
101: ©Peter B. Kaplan, 1986, photo by Eric S. Cohen
102: (top) ©Peter B. Kaplan, 1986, photo by Susan B. Cummings; (bottom) ©Peter B. Kaplan, 1986, photo by J. Stephen Hall
103: (top) Barbara Baumann, 1986, Peter B. Kaplan Images, Ltd.; (bottom) ©Peter B. Kaplan, 1986
104: ©Peter B. Kaplan, 1986, photo by Eric S. Cohen
105: (top) ©Peter B. Kaplan, 1986, photo by Eric S. Cohen; (bottom) ©Laura M. Mueller, 1986, Peter B. Kaplan Images, Ltd.
106: ©Peter B. Kaplan, 1986
111: ©Peter B. Kaplan, 1986

Peter B. Kaplan Images, Ltd. gratefully acknowledges the generous assistance provided by Eastman Kodak Co.

Typesetting by Type Design, Norwalk, Connecticut
Color separations, printing and binding by
R.R. Donnelley & Sons Company, Chicago, Illinois